THE STORY OF
THE LITTLE CHURCH MICE

Phyllis Constant Didleau
Illustrated by Gretchen Gackstatter

BOOK BOOK²

P.O. Box 60144
Colorado Springs, Colorado 80560

The Story of the Little Church Mice
First edition, August 1, 2024
Original illustrations in watercolor by Gretchen Gackstatter

Published by BOOK BOOK SQUARED
P.O. Box 60144
Colorado Springs, Colorado 80960

Published in the United States of America

ISBN: 978-1-943829-59-0

www.goldenrulemasterpieces.com
BOOK BOOK SQUARED is an imprint of Rhyolite Press, LLC

Other books by Phyllis Constant Didleau
and illustrated by Gretchen Gackstatter:

The Little Manger Mouse
The Resurrection Mouse
The Little Church Bird

Once upon a time in the very fertile, abundant, mid-western corn fields, a little country church stood. Its white frame and tall steeple gave the appearance of a great white angel standing among the productive fields.

1

Inside the church and right up front near the pulpit and about fifteen feet from the old upright piano, a family of church mice made their home. They were unseen by all the people of the church—the congragation.

They found a hole in the old tattered carpet that was just the right size to raise all the mice children, until they were big enough to leave home, of course. First they decided that each mouse would take a stand at various points around the sanctuary.

Their mission was one of protection. They pledged with all their heart never to scare the skittish young women. The piano was definitely off-limits. Chewing on felt key pegs was not allowed.

That is why they wanted no other mice in their church who didn't realize the sanctity of their and God's home. No dedicated church mouse would ever chew on Bibles or sacred music. They had rules to respect all areas of the sanctuary.

Next, they voted to disappear under the carpet and remain quiet as a mouse at Sunday morning Service. They could hear the deep bass voice of the farmers lifting up thankful praise to their Lord.

After all, farmers knew better than any worker that their livelihood was provided by their Father in heaven. They knew more than anyone the law of sowing and reaping. For them Sunday was a day of thanksgiving for the bountiful harvest yet to come.

They heard the little children singing "Jesus Loves Me" as their Sunday School lesson began. They could smell the fragrance of the cooking from the kitchen as the farmer's wives began preparing the after service "come one, come all" dinner. And they listened to that old preacher, oh, how they listened!

He told about a man named Jesus who loved us so much he died that we might live forever. That old preacher would lay it on the line. He didn't tickle anybody's ears.

That is what brought people from far and wide. They liked to hear the truth. The mice even saw one high school girl riding her horse to church. She would tether the horse out under the shade tree and sing and teach with her little Sunday School class.

They loved Sunday mornings. Oh, how they loved it. They'd scamper downstairs after service. They had the best meal from all those special Sunday dinners! No one ever saw them. They were polite, neat, tidy, clean little varmints.

When the final prayer was said for dismissal, everyone bade goodbye to one another and left with the love of God stirred within them. They all left with a mission: To raise Godly children, to praise God daily, to love their neighbor and to bring their first fruits into the storehouse next Sunday.

The church mice would scurry back upstairs, scamper to the hole in the carpet and busy themselves about their mission.

And to this day it has been said that in that particular church, not one Bible was chewed on, not one hymnal was destroyed and no problem ever beset the piano. It was said that of all the churches in the country this church must have had special protection. The rumor was that maybe, just maybe, even the church mice prayed, sang and listened to that old preacher!

The End

The Story of the Little Church Mice
—— Review ——

1. What is a pulpit?

a. a step
b. a speaker's box
c. a platform

2. What is a mission?

a. an animal
b. a strong call to work
c. a step stool

3. What does it mean to sow and reap?

a. to make clothing
b. to plant and harvest
c. to run and rest

4. Who is Jesus?

a. God's son
b. a man
c. both a and b

5. *Tickle ears*

a. make things sound good
b. scratch with a finger
c. listen to music

6. *What are first fruits?*

a. apples and oranges that grow first
b. the one at the head of the line
c. giving God the best you have before giving to others

7. *What is a storehouse in the Bible?*

a. the Church
b. your house
c. a garage

8. *What is a sanctuary?*

a. a yard
b. the parking lot
c. a place of rest and safety

9. *What is a Sunday School?*

a. a church time for children
b. a place to learn to play
c. a swimming pool

10. The people left the church with a mission. What was it?

a. to bring first fruits into the storehouse.

b. to raise Godly children

c. to praise God daily

d. to love their neighbor

e. all of the above

About Hazel Dell Methodist Church

The author attended Hazel Dell Methodist Church near Council Bluffs, Iowa in the 1950s. This story is based on her fond memories of this little country church.

Reverend Floyd Aldrich and his wife were retired missionaries who had served forty years in India. Afterward, wishing to continue serving the Lord, they found pastoring at Hazel Dell Church an ideal calling.

Stained glass windows on the south wall are a memorial to the author's parents, Herbert & Harriett Constant. Generations of her family attended Hazel Dell Methodist Church and now lie in rest at the church's cemetary.

Phyllis holds a bachelor Degree with a Life Certificate in elementary education from the University of Northern Colorado in Greeley. Her Biblical studies include a two-year course from the Institute of Theology by Extension through the Department of International Studies, Open Bible Churches.

About the illustrator

Gretchen Gackstatter received a Bachelor Degree in Fine Arts from the University of Northern Colorado. She is an award-winning watercolor artist and art teacher currently based in Belleville, Illinois.

She has a passion for plein air painting and feels her artwork is fully complimented when embraced by nature. Gretchen's writing and artwork compliment one another. Her profound insight of life's joys and tragedies are artfully reflected in both her writings and paintings. See more of her amazing work on her website: GGwatercolor.com.

www.ingramcontent.com/pod-product-compliance
Lightning Source LLC
LaVergne TN
LVHW070839080426
835512LV00025B/3486

*9 7 8 1 9 4 3 8 2 9 5 9 0 *